THIS IS ME

THE ME I CHOOSE TO BE

WORKBOOK

Greatness Journey
EMPOWER YOUR CHILD

WRITE.RECITE.REPEAT SCRIPTS
PLUS COLORING PAGES FOR YOUR CHILD

RYAN & JANUARY DONOVAN

DISCLAIMER. We are not child psychologists or psychiatrists. Content provided is for self-development purposes and does not take the place of professional advice. Every effort has been made to ensure that all information included in this book is accurate and helpful to our readers at the time of publishing.

No liability is assumed for losses or damages resulting from the reader's personal application. You are accountable for your own actions and choices. Write to the publisher for specific questions regarding this disclaimer.

"Our self image, strongly held, essentially determines what we become."

~ Maxwell Maltz

Greatness Journey

EMPOWER YOUR CHILD

This workbook is dedicated to our children:
Jack Ryan, Pia, Ena, Bo, Ifa, and Vivi.
May you become a light to this world and
choose a life of Greatness.

—————～—————

AMDG

We thank God for his abundant love and mercy.

May our work lead souls to his divine adventure, and

may his light be the guiding path for all our children.

WE BELIEVE THAT THE ULTIMATE GREATNESS JOURNEY

IS THE JOURNEY WE TAKE TOWARDS THE DIVINE.

"The greatest discovery of my generation is that human beings can alter their lives by altering their attitudes of mind."
~ William James

"It's the repetition of affirmations that leads to belief. And once that belief becomes a deep conviction, things begin to happen."
~ Claude M. Bristol

ABOUT THE AUTHORS

Ryan & January

Ryan and January Donovan - entrepreneurs; podcast hosts; parents of six wonderful children; and creators of Greatness Journey, a mindset education company which provides helpful tools in empowering children to achieve their greatness.

Besides having a strong pulse in business, both husband and wife share a passion for contributing value to the world. Despite all the external influences that pose a threat to modern-day families, Ryan and January remain steadfast in raising their children intentionally so they'd grow with the same noble mission as their parents to create a positive impact and to gently touch the lives of others around them.

Ryan is a certified mindset trainer and coach, who has run several successful businesses. Meanwhile, January is a self-worth strategist with two decades of experience in training women on essential life skills. They have been married for 12 years now yet Ryan still enjoys to take his wife out on dates every Friday night.

Though they have already accomplished so much, both believe that they're still in the process of becoming the best version of themselves. They have always been relentless learners and dreamers and as their family grows, so do their goals and dreams.

CONTENTS

INTRODUCTION

The vision behind this SELF IMAGE STATEMENT Workbook is to help you design your child's Self Image before the world defines it for them. We have a self image crisis in our culture and if we are not deliberate about teaching our children how to see themselves, being worthy of good, then we risk having the world dictate how they should see themselves. Our goal is to help them see for themselves the best that they can be.

By intentionally putting these words into their conscious mind they can develop an awareness of the 'me' they choose to be. Their choice of words are powerful indicators of how they view themselves; their words will become flesh! Words are extremely powerful tools. This workbook will guide you to choose words that will EMPOWER and EQUIP your child to believe in themselves.

Through repetition these words will take root into the subconscious mind and form a habit. These habits are called paradigms. Paradigms are a multitude of habits that dictate our behaviors and cause our decisions. Cultivating your child's subconscious mindset to see themselves as strong, confident and valuable will build their resilience from negative influences.

We live in a culture that bombards our self worth, it is our duty as parents to be proactive about designing the image they hold of themselves. Through repetition, this book is designed to help shape your child's self image. Ultimately, their self image will largely determine how far they will go in life.

NOTE TO PARENTS

Cheers to awesome parents like you!

Fast forward 30 years from now. What tools would you wish you had given your children so they could build their dreams sooner? This may be a tough question to answer at this stage, but asking this question allows us to reflect on how we are proactively preparing our children to live great lives.

This is what '*Greatness Journey*' is about.
It's about equipping your child's toolbox with empowering tools that will help them maximize their full potential and become CONFIDENT in chasing their dreams.

But HOW do we prepare our children?

WE BEGIN WITH BUILDING THEIR FOUNDATION.
We train their mindset and equip them with the skill set they need to become resilient and self-confident.
We give them empowering words (called scripts) as foundational tools for their minds.

Words matter!
How they talk to themselves will determine the quality of their lives, so it truly does matter.

Write, Recite, Repeat!
Write: Rewriting scripts by hand is one of the most effective ways to program and retain new information. This stimulates a part of your brain known as the RAS (Reticular Activating System). The RAS acts as a filter for everything your brain needs to process. It literally helps you focus, and we know what you focus on expands. In *Write It Down, Make It Happen*, writing consultant Henriette Anne Klauser says, "Writing triggers the RAS, which in turn sends a signal to the cerebral cortex: Wake up! Pay attention! Don't miss this detail!"

Recite: Reciting the scripts as often as possible helps to ingrain a reflex response in situations. Reciting with emphasis and passion will get more emotion behind what you are saying. Emotion creates motion!

Repeat: By repeating the scripts through writing and reciting, you are implanting new words and thoughts into the subconscious mind. This will help you to memorize and, more importantly, internalize these scripts. When you repeat, you remember. This will help change paradigms and in turn increase confidence!

Training children to write, recite, and repeat these self image scripts will cultivate their resiliency skills and help build confidence.
These positive mental habits will become the lens through which they view the world.

Cheers to all our children!

Welcome to the Greatness Journey.

Onward and upward towards greatness,

Ryan & January

QUICK STORY

Jack, a 10-year-old boy, had been dreaming of an amazing treehouse ever since he could remember. He found the perfect tree in his backyard to build this dream. He saved up his money to buy all the materials for this epic tree house.

Finally, it was time to begin.
He opened his toolbox, and all he saw were three nails, an ax, and a broken hammer.

That's it…

Those were the only tools he had to build his dream.

Jack thought to himself, "How could I build a treehouse with only three nails, an ax, and a broken hammer?

Even if I wanted to, I wouldn't know how to with the tools I've got."

He quit before he even got started.

He quit because he didn't have enough tools in his toolbox.

Affirmations are tools... help your child fill their tool box.

HOW TO USE THIS WORKBOOK

This is *not* your ordinary book. Its purpose is to develop your children's mental habits through repetition, but in a *fun and creative way*. Since it is intended to be used often, place this book on a *visible spot* that is easy for children to reach when asked to pick a script of the day or week.

As soon as they have chosen a statement, work with them so it can be ingrained *effectively* into their minds. Have them recite it to you as part of their daily commitment. Make it fun by saying it together, with emphasis and passion. Better yet, try singing their selected script at times. There are also parts of this book which they can *color and scribble on*. Encourage their creativity -- let it run wild!

Your task as parents is to keep the entire process fun, to hold them accountable, and to provide real-life examples of how they can apply the script into their own lives. Guide them but leave a little room for their independence to grow.

WHAT IS A SCRIPT?

A script is a guided phrase or sentence that helps program your response in certain situations. Repeating these statements impresses them into the subconscious mind and over time, your belief in them strengthens -- causing change in the way you think and ultimately, in the way you act.

When your children write, recite, repeat, and color these scripts, their mindset gradually grows in preparation for the big world -- where they will chase their dreams and find their own greatness.

Step 1:
Read each page with your children. Engage them in a brief conversation about their thoughts, or ask them to color a page and the script to build awareness.

Step 2:
Encourage them to focus on one script per day or week. Get them familiar with the words, as well as the "write, recite, repeat" process.

Step 3:
Place this book on a visible location, like on top of a night stand, coffee table, or a "special chair," then form the habit of letting your children work on their chosen script every day.

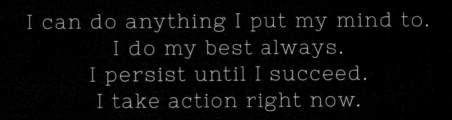

This Is Me

I can do anything I put my mind to.
I do my best always.
I persist until I succeed.
I take action right now.

I learn something new every day.
I grow from my mistakes.
It doesn't matter what anyone says,
I do what is right.
I trust my decisions.
I respect my body.
I honor myself.

I believe in my dreams.
I was born for a purpose.
I choose to laugh.
I choose peace.
I choose hope.

I choose to see what is beautiful
in this world.

I am worthy of love.
I am brave.
I am kind.
I am healthy.
I am fun.
I am free.

This Is Me:

(your name)

I CAN DO ANYTHING I PUT MY MIND TO

Color the scripts!

WRITE. RECITE. REPEAT

1. _____

2. _____

3. _____

4. _____

5. _____

6. _____

7. _____

8. _____

9. _____

10. _____

I DO MY BEST ALWAYS

WRITE. RECITE. REPEAT

1. _____

2. _____

3. _____

4. _____

5. _____

6. _____

7. _____

8. _____

9. _____

10. _____

I PERSIST UNTIL I SUCCEED

WRITE. RECITE. REPEAT

1. _____

2. _____

3. _____

4. _____

5. _____

6. _____

7. _____

8. _____

9. _____

10. _____

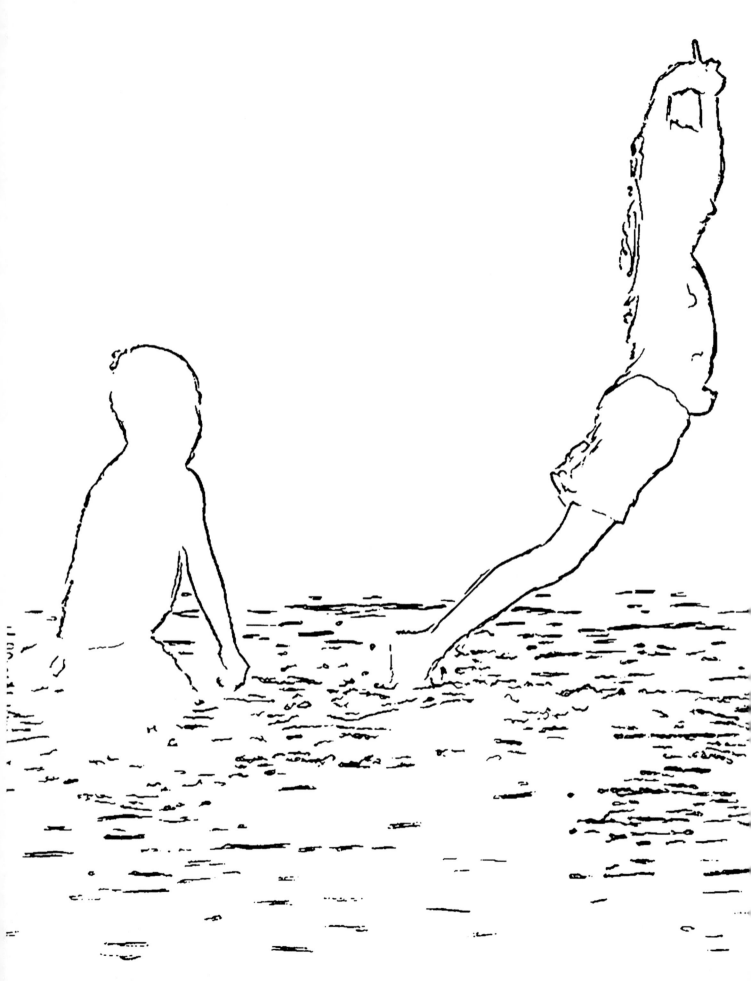

I TAKE ACTION RIGHT NOW

WRITE. RECITE. REPEAT

1. _____

2. _____

3. _____

4. _____

5. _____

6. _____

7. _____

8. _____

9. _____

10. _____

I LEARN SOMETHING NEW EVERY DAY

WRITE. RECITE. REPEAT

1. _____

2. _____

3. _____

4. _____

5. _____

6. _____

7. _____

8. _____

9. _____

10. _____

I GROW FROM MY MISTAKES

WRITE. RECITE. REPEAT

1. _____

2. _____

3. _____

4. _____

5. _____

6. _____

7. _____

8. _____

9. _____

10. _____

IT DOESN'T MATTER WHAT ANYONE SAYS; I DO WHAT IS RIGHT

WRITE. RECITE. REPEAT

1. _____

2. _____

3. _____

4. _____

5. _____

6. _____

7. _____

8. _____

9. _____

10. _____

I TRUST MY DECISIONS

WRITE. RECITE. REPEAT

1. _____

2. _____

3. _____

4. _____

5. _____

6. _____

7. _____

8. _____

9. _____

10. _____

I RESPECT MY BODY

WRITE. RECITE. REPEAT

1. _____

2. _____

3. _____

4. _____

5. _____

6. _____

7. _____

8. _____

9. _____

10. _____

I HONOR MYSELF

WRITE. RECITE. REPEAT

1. _____

2. _____

3. _____

4. _____

5. _____

6. _____

7. _____

8. _____

9. _____

10. _____

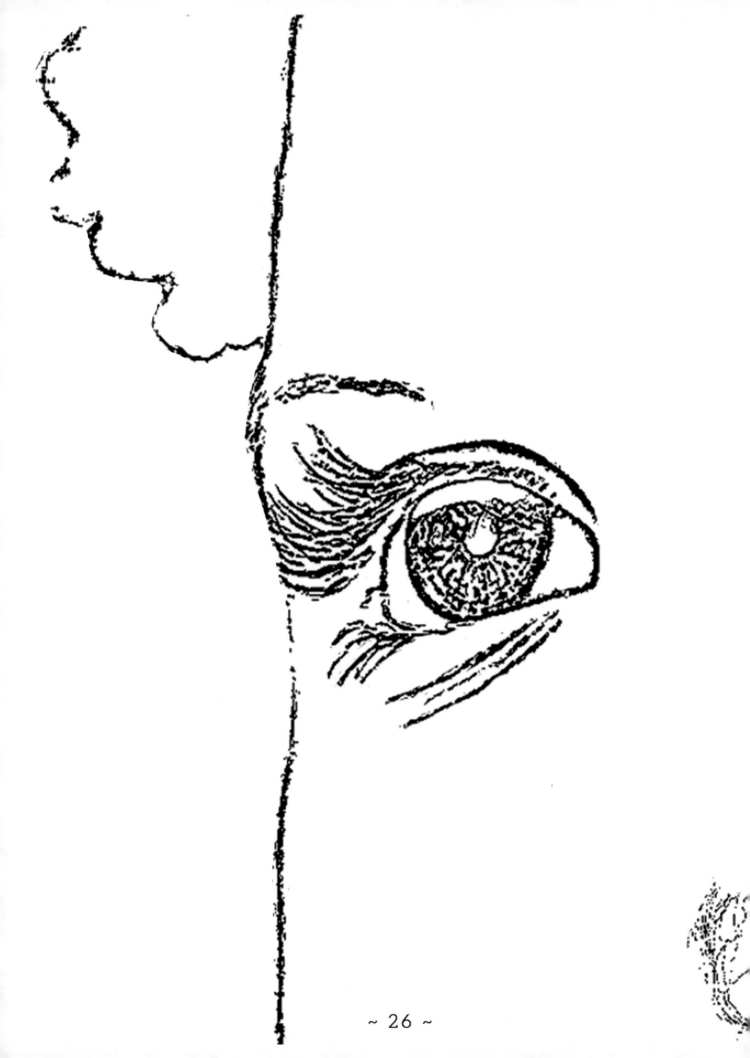

I BELIEVE IN MY DREAMS

WRITE. RECITE. REPEAT

1. _____

2. _____

3. _____

4. _____

5. _____

6. _____

7. _____

8. _____

9. _____

10. _____

I WAS BORN FOR A PURPOSE

WRITE. RECITE. REPEAT

1. _____

2. _____

3. _____

4. _____

5. _____

6. _____

7. _____

8. _____

9. _____

10. _____

I CHOOSE TO LAUGH

WRITE. RECITE. REPEAT

1. _____

2. _____

3. _____

4. _____

5. _____

6. _____

7. _____

8. _____

9. _____

10. _____

I CHOOSE PEACE

WRITE. RECITE. REPEAT

1. _____

2. _____

3. _____

4. _____

5. _____

6. _____

7. _____

8. _____

9. _____

10. _____

I CHOOSE HOPE

WRITE. RECITE. REPEAT

1. _____

2. _____

3. _____

4. _____

5. _____

6. _____

7. _____

8. _____

9. _____

10. _____

I CHOOSE TO SEE WHAT IS BEAUTIFUL IN THIS WORLD

WRITE. RECITE. REPEAT

1. _____

2. _____

3. _____

4. _____

5. _____

6. _____

7. _____

8. _____

9. _____

10. _____

I AM WORTHY OF LOVE

WRITE. RECITE. REPEAT

1. _____

2. _____

3. _____

4. _____

5. _____

6. _____

7. _____

8. _____

9. _____

10. _____

I AM BRAVE

WRITE. RECITE. REPEAT

1. _____

2. _____

3. _____

4. _____

5. _____

6. _____

7. _____

8. _____

9. _____

10. _____

I AM KIND

WRITE. RECITE. REPEAT

1. _____

2. _____

3. _____

4. _____

5. _____

6. _____

7. _____

8. _____

9. _____

10. _____

~ 44

I AM HEALTHY

WRITE. RECITE. REPEAT

1. _____

2. _____

3. _____

4. _____

5. _____

6. _____

7. _____

8. _____

9. _____

10. _____

I AM FUN

WRITE. RECITE. REPEAT

1. _____

2. _____

3. _____

4. _____

5. _____

6. _____

7. _____

8. _____

9. _____

10. _____

I AM FREE

WRITE. RECITE. REPEAT

1. _____

2. _____

3. _____

4. _____

5. _____

6. _____

7. _____

8. _____

9. _____

10. _____

THIS IS ME

Greatness Journey
EMPOWER YOUR CHILD

CLOSING THOUGHTS

You have the power to choose to become your BEST YOU.
You are responsible.
You are beautiful, and you are good.
Who you become is a choice and a privilege.

At every moment, you can learn to become
the best that you can be.
You are free to grow, you are free to fall, you are free to learn,
you are free to choose whoever you want to be.

You have a purpose, you have a choice, and
both matter to the world, because the world needs you.

The world needs your light.
The world needs your voice.
The world needs you to make a WISE choice.

You can choose who you want to be; that's what makes you free.
You can create something meaningful, something remarkable.
You can dream of the impossible and work hard toward your
highest goal.

You can design the world you choose.

You can choose hope.
You can choose love.
You can choose peace.
You can choose to see what is good in this world.

You are free to respond; that is a choice.
You are free to choose the YOU you want to be.

You get to DECIDE the YOU you want to be.
This is you!

Greatness Journey

EMPOWER YOUR CHILD

Donovan Creed

I can do anything I put my *Mind* to

I can do all things through *Christ* who strengthens m[e]

I do my *Best* always

I learn something new *Everyday*

I take action right *Now*

I *Persist* until I succeed

It doesn't matter what anyone says – I do what's *Rig[ht]*

I'm not afraid *Jesus* is with me every where I go

I can, I will, I must – be a *Saint*

*J*ESUS I TRUST IN YOU

May your children be the light that the world needs now.

Cheers from our family to yours,

The Donovans

Made in the USA
Monee, IL
21 January 2022